From Conflict to Clarity

Winning A High-Conflict Divorce

By: Edwin B. Gray

Hardback- ISBN: 979-8-9901713-7-4

Published by: It Was A Dark And Starry Night

Printed in the United States of America

First Edition: 2025

For permissions requests and interviews, please contact:

It Was A Dark And Starry Night LLC.

OBO B. L. Davidson

5900 Balcones Dr.

Austin, TX 78731

Table of Contents

Introduction

❖••━━━━••••━━━━••❖

If you're reading this book, you've probably found yourself in a place you never imagined when you got married. According to the Pew Research Center, in 2019, the United States had the highest rate of children living in single-parent homes out of 130 countries. Maybe you're just starting to consider divorce, or perhaps you're doing research because you see your marriage falling apart despite your best efforts to make it work. Either way, this book is here as a tool—a guide to help you navigate divorce with concise, practical advice to stay legally compliant, well-prepared, and emotionally grounded throughout the process.

A little history about my own marriage: I was married for almost 14 years before the divorce process began. The custody battle lasted a year, followed by a four-year modification process that started less than two years later. The original trial was presided over by a judge, but for the modification, my ex-wife requested a jury trial. I won both cases. The divorce was incredibly contentious—an emotionally charged fight centered around custody and other disputes. We share four children: three daughters and one son.

Now, pause for a moment and think about that. In a state as traditionally conservative as Texas, a father was granted custody of his four children—not once, but twice.

And let me address any assumptions you might be making: my ex-wife wasn't a drug addict or unfit. She was, in fact, a senior business professional at a Fortune 10 company. This wasn't about her being incapable; it was about what was best for our children.

This book isn't just about my story; it's about helping you face your own challenges and equipping you with the tools you need to navigate them. During my divorce proceedings, I encountered several people who were either going through a divorce themselves or contemplating one. They often came to me for advice on how to handle specific situations in their cases. Over time, they started calling me the "Divorce Whisperer" because I would share what I had learned from my own experience. Many of them would take my suggestions to their lawyers and later tell me my advice was spot on.

Eventually, they challenged me to write this book to help others navigate what is often the most difficult experience of their lives. After spending more than six years in the legal system, I became deeply familiar with the dos and don'ts of the process. My goal is to help you avoid potential pitfalls that could jeopardize your custody chances—whether you have children or not. These principles apply across different demographics and court proceedings.

Every divorce is unique, but I noticed recurring themes in the areas of contention, whether the divorces involved children or not. Some of the most common questions people asked me included:

1. How do you maintain your integrity in a system that doesn't value integrity?
2. How do you parent with someone who has no desire to parent with you?
3. How do you not let hate to take over your heart when you are constantly bombarded internally with thoughts of accusation against your former spouse?
4. How do you maintain the mental health of your children who are going through divorce with you?
5. How do you communicate with them about your children so their emotional and psychological growth isn't stunted?
6. What clinical tools and strategies do you use to engage with your former spouse?
7. Will it ever get any better?

Over the next few chapters, I'll tackle these topics and more. I'm going to give you some hard truths—things that might make you uncomfortable—but these lessons were pivotal in the decisions that led to my success. I'll say things that challenge conventional wisdom, and yes, I might even say things that make you mutter a curse or two under your breath. But trust me, everything I share comes from hundreds of hours of counseling, mentorship, and life experience as a man navigating the legal system while fighting for his children.

If you're willing to think outside the box and push yourself, you'll emerge as a stronger, better version of yourself. More importantly, your legacy—your child or children—will benefit by becoming healthier and happier. If you're serious about your future and the future of your children, grab a pen, a highlighter, and your web browser. These tools will be essential for finding local resources and exploring materials to help you grow. Throughout this book, I'll introduce you to what I call HOT topics—Honest, Open, and Transparent truths. I can tell you with absolute certainty that these strategies and principles work.

I learned how to let the best version of myself shine, even in the worst situations. If that's something you believe is worth your time and effort, then let's begin.

Chapter 1
Read the Divorce Paperwork Thoroughly

⊱⊱‖‖————•●•————‖‖⊰⊰

W hen you're going through a divorce—or even just considering one—this is one of the first things you should research. If I could go back, understanding this would have been the smartest investment I made at the start of my divorce.

In Texas, there are three types of orders to be aware of: standing orders, temporary orders, and restraining orders. Standing orders come into effect automatically when a case is filed and remain in place until a judge issues a different ruling, such as temporary restraining orders, temporary orders, or any other specific set of rules to govern the divorce process. It's important to note that not every county in Texas has standing orders, and not every state uses them either. Regardless of the type of order, it's absolutely essential to read them thoroughly. These orders have two significant impacts on you and your case, and understanding them from the outset can make all the difference.

First, the orders outline what is expected of you and define what is legally permissible. In my county, even minor missteps can lead to serious trouble. Here are a few examples: parents cannot disrupt the children's lives physically or emotionally; you cannot disparage the other parent to the children; opening or diverting the other party's mail is prohibited; and rules also govern the money you withdraw from joint accounts and how you handle insurance policies. To protect yourself and avoid unintentionally harming your case, read these documents thoroughly. Search for family law and orders specific to your county and state to understand what is permitted where you live. Breaking these rules, even unknowingly, can damage your case. A skilled lawyer can use any violation against you on the witness stand, painting you as deceptive or spiteful. Don't give them that chance—know the rules and follow them.

Second, these orders apply equally to your ex-spouse. If they violate any of the outlined rules, you have legal recourse. You can petition the court to hold them in contempt or request the judge to amend the order in your favor. However, judges strongly dislike frivolous claims, so it's important to have multiple or extreme examples of rule-breaking, especially when it involves the children. To help document violations, consider using a parenting app like Our Family Wizard, AppClose, or similar tools. These apps allow you to track conversations and interactions. I'll go into more detail on this in the communication section later in the book.

Let me share an example I witnessed firsthand during one of my court hearings. A couple ahead of us was in court discussing violations of their orders. The man had been placed on supervised visitation for disturbing the child's peace. He had been talking about the case and disparaging the mother in front of the child. The divorce was clearly bitter; they couldn't even attend school events together without arguments that required police intervention. This serves as a reminder of how damaging rule-breaking can be, especially when children are involved.

The key takeaway here is simple: read all documents thoroughly. Early in my case, I missed over 40 standing order violations by my ex-spouse. Had I been more vigilant, I could have documented these breaches with photos, dates, times, and detailed descriptions. Proper documentation would have strengthened my case and made it easier for the judge to enforce the rules. Don't make the same mistake I did—stay informed and prepared.

Chapter 2
The Right Lawyer and Your Responses

✦ ▮▮▮————•••————▮▮▮ ✦

C hoosing the right lawyer is the second most important decision you'll make in your case. Over the course of my two cases with my ex-wife, I had the privilege of working with four outstanding lawyers— and two who were, frankly, subpar. When you're sworn in during legal proceedings, you promise to tell the truth, the whole truth, and nothing but the truth. Lawyers, as officers of the court, are held to the same standard. So why, then, do some lawyers lie or present false evidence? The answer lies in a loophole: lawyers ask questions, not provide answers. This gives them the "ability" to present information that may be completely or partially false, as long as they can claim they didn't know it wasn't true.

I personally witnessed two of my ex-wife's lawyers do exactly this. They asked her questions in court that they knew were false—something the discovery documents could have disproven right then and there. Unfortunately, by the time the truth was buried in hundreds of pages of discovery information, the moment had passed. This is why having the right lawyer on your side is crucial. A good lawyer must be able to identify both the strengths and weaknesses of your case. You won't have the time—or capacity—to catch every lie during proceedings, so your lawyer's vigilance is essential. It's easy to find a lawyer willing to bend the truth for you, but that approach won't serve you well in the long run.

For reference, I won two lengthy cases—one lasting over 1.5 years and another spanning three years—by sticking to the truth. You need a lawyer who is ethical, honorable, fiercely dedicated to your case, and most importantly, brutally honest with you. Anything less could cost you dearly.

When you have children, most divorce cases hinge on the concept of "the best interest of the child." That phrase is not just a formality; it's the guiding principle behind many decisions. It's crucial to choose a lawyer who prioritizes what's best for your children even more than what you might think is best for yourself. I know that may sound counterintuitive, but hear me out: divorce is an emotional battle, and you're going to be triggered. In fact, you're likely reading this book because you've already been triggered.

Your honest request to any lawyer should be this: "Tell me what is in the best interest of my children." This approach will help ground you and ensure that the most vulnerable individuals—your kids—come first. During my

9

custody modification, my lawyer, Ms. Sims, frequently reminded me, "Your feelings are valid, but that doesn't mean they align with what's best for the children or what the law requires. You may want X to happen, but we need to prove Y, and even then, it may only lead to A results at best. Do you still want to pursue it?"

This kind of honesty is vital. Some might assume the lawyer is being dismissive or trying to avoid work, but that wasn't the case with Ms. Sims. At one point, I was feeling defeated. I was hemorrhaging money, caring for my mother with cancer, and my ex-wife wasn't helping with out-of-pocket expenses for our children. I was ready to give up and told Ms. Sims to agree to whatever my ex-wife wanted because I couldn't afford to keep fighting. She refused to let me quit, pointing out the long-term consequences for my children. She worked out a payment plan I could manage and reminded me of the bigger picture: splitting custody wasn't in my kids' best interest. Because I listened, my ex-wife's visitation was reduced to standard, her overnight stays during the week were minimized, and her child support increased.

Not all lawyers will go to bat for you this way. I've had a lawyer who took over $10,000 and never filed the necessary paperwork, leaving my case in disarray. This is why you need a lawyer with integrity, one who will separate facts from feelings and guide you toward decisions that benefit your case. In court, your feelings are irrelevant unless supported by tangible evidence. A skilled lawyer will help you focus on what matters most.

Another critical aspect of having the right lawyer is their honesty and integrity. My ex-wife's lawyers were so shaken during the trial that they stopped asking me open-ended questions entirely. They attacked my faith and even introduced evidence they knew was false—something clearly disproven in their own discovery documentation— but they asked the questions anyway. I believe this behavior undermined their credibility with the jury, which contributed to my success. Your responses in court are just as important as your lawyer's strategy. Early on, I told my lawyers I wouldn't lie. If I had done something wrong, I wanted to admit it upfront. Many people try to project an image of perfection, but let's face it: very few divorces happen without fault on both sides. If you've made mistakes, admit them. Here's why: admitting your faults removes the possibility of a "gotcha" moment during cross-examination. I've seen judges become visibly angry when someone was caught telling half-truths. When it was my turn, I openly admitted my faults to the point that I joked afterward about needing witness protection.

This transparency had a profound effect. My ex-wife's attorney didn't repeat any questions from my original testimony or counter my statements with conflicting evidence. In contrast, my ex-wife's testimony was riddled with contradictions that were quickly refuted by evidence. I could see the subtle shifts in the judge's demeanor, and it was clear that my candid responses carried more weight than her lack of candor.

Jury reactions also matter. As the plaintiff in the modification case, I testified first. During cross-

11

examination, opposing counsel wanted me to answer only "yes" or "no," avoiding any context or explanation. But the truth is, not all answers are that simple. When I needed to elaborate, I found ways to signal my lawyer that I had more to say, which allowed them to redirect me later. Sometimes I'd answer both "yes" and "no" to force clarification or say the opposite of what opposing counsel wanted. This strategy ensured that my side of the story was heard while maintaining credibility.

Ultimately, the right lawyer will not only fight for your case but also prepare you to present yourself honestly and effectively. Their guidance can be the difference between success and failure in court.

Here's an example of an exchange during our engagement:

Her lawyer asked, "Mr. Gray, do you think it is best for the child to have a relationship with their mother?"

I answered, "No."

She followed up, "So you don't think they should engage with their mother?"

Again, I replied, "No."

Then she asked, "Why?"

This was my chance to give a full, detailed answer. I took it. My response was so thorough that the lawyer tried to object, but the judge quickly reminded her that she had asked the "why" question. After this happened multiple times, the lawyer stopped asking me "why" questions altogether and just accepted whatever answer I gave.

When my ex-wife testified, I paid close attention to how the jury reacted. Every time she said, "I don't recall" or gave a false answer, my lawyer would present evidence to contradict her. The jury's body language and facial expressions made it clear they didn't believe her. That said, she's attractive and cried through about 50% of her time on the stand. I even noticed a few women on the jury crying along with her.

However, her attitude toward my lawyers was callous, curt, and outright rude. In contrast, my demeanor remained consistent whether I was addressing her lawyers or my own. The difference was so noticeable that, during closing arguments, her lawyer tried to address it, saying to the jury, "Yes, he's very articulate and personable, and my client isn't as much—but don't let his articulateness fool you." This moment solidified for me how important demeanor, honesty, and consistency are in the courtroom. It wasn't just about the facts; it was about how those facts were presented.

Your demeanor and attitude in court play a crucial role in your success. However, I'll admit there was one area where I needed to grow. I had a tendency to let my frustration and disgust show on my face when I wasn't testifying. When something was clearly a lie, it took every ounce of self-control not to stand up and call it out. Although I didn't physically react, my body language betrayed me.

It's important to find a balance. You can't be a robot, as that will come across as inauthentic, but you also can't be overly emotional, as it will reflect poorly on you. During the five days of my jury trial, I learned to manage my reactions. I would put my head down, shake it subtly, or jot down my thoughts. Writing helped me refocus and even reminded me to check our parenting communication records for evidence that could counter her claims.

On multiple occasions, I was able to identify evidence that directly contradicted her testimony. Staying composed and focused on the truth allowed me to maintain credibility in the courtroom. In essence, my advice is this: stay focused on the truth. I believe this approach was one of the key factors that helped me win both of my cases.

One more thing: make sure to track your assets meticulously. This will also play a significant role in protecting your interests during the divorce process.

Chapter 3
Division of Assets

❖·—————··—————·❖

Money is one of the most contentious aspects of divorce, and for good reason. It drives actions and words that often stray far beyond the bounds of normal conscience. As the saying goes, *the love of money is the root of all kinds of evil.* Just as some people will do anything for love, others will do anything for money—including entering a marriage with that very goal in mind. For some, the assets you've accumulated are the main attraction.

Unless you're independently wealthy or have substantial personal assets already established, this may not apply to you. For most people, marriage is about building a life together, with both spouses contributing to their household's growth. Whether one spouse earned more or less, in most cases, both played a role in accumulating shared assets. However, during a divorce, the love of money—and bitterness toward your former spouse—can cloud judgment and drive harmful behaviors.

15

According to a 2023 article in *Forbes Magazine*, nearly 50% of first marriages end in divorce, followed by 60% of second marriages and 70% of third marriages. You are not alone in this journey, and like many others, you'll face the challenge of dividing assets. Almost half of all divorces involve this crucial and often contentious step.

Here are a few questions to consider when thinking about the wealth you and your spouse have built together:

1. How many assets do you have?
2. What is your personal value of the assets?
3. What type of state do you live in?
4. Do you know about all the assets?
5. What is your level of communication with your former spouse?

We often wish divorce could be as simple as dividing fruit: "I'll take all my apples, you take all your oranges, and we'll go our separate ways." Unfortunately, if you're reading this manual, it's likely because your divorce is—or you expect it to be—contentious. Effective planning can save you significant time, stress, and frustration.

My first suggestion is to open separate accounts to keep an accurate record of your resources and split the bills fairly. If you're still using a joint account, your former partner could potentially spend or hide money, leaving you with the burden of proving what you actually contributed or spent. While hiding assets is illegal, it's a tactic often used in contentious divorces.

By having your own account, you can protect yourself from accusations of "misappropriating funds" and maintain transparency. Additionally, most states have specific rules regarding the use of community and personal funds during a divorce. Understanding and adhering to these rules will help you navigate the process more smoothly and avoid unnecessary complications.

Texas is a community property state, meaning that most assets acquired during the marriage are considered jointly owned and will be split equitably during a divorce. In contrast, states like North Dakota separate personal and community property. Typically, in community property states, anything you owned before marriage remains yours, and anything your spouse owned prior to marriage remains theirs. However, shared assets, such as a home, can be one of the most challenging hurdles to overcome. It's wise to start planning how to divide major assets like a home as early as possible. Take, for example, my best friend and his first wife. They were married for about four years, had no children, and separated before ultimately divorcing. While their divorce process lasted several months, the longest and most contentious part was dividing their home. If you want to keep the home, you'll need to compensate your spouse for their share of the home's equity. Though it was an emotionally bitter experience, they managed to divide their assets and haven't spoken personally since that day, almost 16 years ago.

On the other hand, I know a friend from church whose spouse caused significant financial hardship by withdrawing money from the family account for personal use. This left the managing spouse and their children struggling, while the other spouse still wanted half of all assets. My advice to them was to itemize everything—document all assets, including those taken without prior knowledge. This prevented the other spouse from hiding or selling items that belonged to the family.

One of my own mistakes was failing to itemize assets before leaving the home. Many items were removed, sold, or hidden to prevent me from claiming them. From that experience, I began advising people to create a detailed inventory. Itemization should include photos with dates and locations. Remember, hiding assets is illegal, and if items are sold during divorce proceedings, you're entitled to half of the selling price in most cases.

To make asset division smoother, you and your spouse can start choosing what each of you wants ahead of time. If disagreements arise, the court may use an alternating selection method. This process typically works as follows: one person chooses, then the other, and so on, alternating turns. To avoid one party taking all the "best" items, the pattern often switches: she chooses, he chooses, he chooses, she chooses, and so on. If hostility is an issue, you can request this method through the judge to keep the process fair and orderly.

Here's another example of asset division: A coworker of mine had been separated from her husband for three years. She moved from Arizona, a community property state, to a state in the East. Before the marriage, she owned a home in Arizona, which would typically be considered personal property. However, her husband later demanded half of the future sale of that home. After consulting an Arizona lawyer, she was reassured that her home was not community property under state law. This highlights another critical point: always get a second opinion, even from lawyers. In your circle, there's likely someone who knows or can recommend a family law attorney. Getting sound advice could save you—or add—hundreds of thousands of dollars.

The next chapter focuses on those with children: how to divide your time with them. It's a critical and often emotional topic, but careful planning can make all the difference. Let's dive in.

Chapter 4
Help for Myself

ow that we've addressed some of the logistical
and legal aspects of divorce, let's focus on
something even more important—what will last
long after your divorce: your sanity. A wise person
recognizes that rebuilding themselves is essential. You've
just ended 2, 10, 20, or even 30 years of your life with
another person, and if you think you're going to be fine
without reflection or healing, you're setting yourself up
for failure.

If you don't have children, odds are you'll eventually
begin dating again. Statistics show that many people
remarry at least once after divorce. I firmly believe many
second marriages fail because individuals don't take the
time to heal properly after their first marriage. Think about
it: you've adapted to living with someone else's habits,
likes, and dislikes, and that has shaped you. Divorce
requires you to unlearn negative habits, heal emotionally,

and rebuild your identity outside of your previous relationship.

Through my divorce and conversations with associates, lawyers, family counselors, and a parental facilitator, I've identified key areas you must address for personal growth. These areas dramatically affect not only your health but also the well-being of your children if you have them. Dr. Linda Rollins-Threats, my parental facilitator with over 40 years of experience helping families navigate high-conflict divorces, introduced me to the concept of the sphere of control. She encouraged us to stretch our arms out as far as we could. "Everything within your reach," she explained, "represents what you can control." It was a minor epiphany for me. Even if someone is within your reach—physically or emotionally—you're not controlling them, only manipulating them.

High-conflict divorces present countless opportunities for manipulation. Whether it's using children's emotions, their activities, or sensitive subjects, the urge to elicit a reaction can be strong. Instead of falling into this trap, focus on self-improvement.

Here are four critical questions to guide your growth:

1. How did I contribute to the downfall of my marriage?
2. What negative habits did I learn while married?
3. Why am I so bitter toward my ex-spouse?

What can I control in the divorce process? (This will be discussed in more depth in the chapter "Fighting Fair.")

Addressing these questions requires brutal honesty. You must be willing to confront the role you played and the actions you allowed. To show you what I mean, I'll be transparent about my own journey. I was unfaithful to my wife. Why? Because I felt a lack of self-worth and physical intimacy. Compounding this, I was a victim of domestic abuse for years. As a man, this was one of the hardest things for me to reconcile.

Was I being beaten mercilessly? No. But I endured physical blows and other forms of abuse that caused lasting emotional damage. I kept thinking, *No one will believe me. Why didn't you leave? Why didn't you stop her?* But to stop her, I would have had to hit her back, and if I left, I risked losing custody of my children. I decided to communicate my emotions with words, not violence. At 6'6" and 250 pounds, I knew how I might be perceived. Even when I sought help, I was immediately sent to a class for domestic violence offenders—not victims—without anyone asking why I was there. The stigma that men are always the abusers completely ignores the reality that abuse is more than physical. Through this experience, I learned that domestic violence encompasses emotional, psychological, and physical harm.

This journey of self-reflection and understanding is difficult but necessary. It's the first step toward reclaiming your identity and creating a healthier, stronger version of yourself for the future. After experiencing these issues, I was conditioned to believe I was less than, that I couldn't win, and that it was better to suffer with my children than without them. Abuse can take many forms—verbal, emotional, physical, or sexual. Being constantly put down, spoken to in a demeaning manner, or having physical intimacy weaponized as a form of punishment are all elements of domestic violence.

People often say, *words don't hurt*, but legally, there is a concept called "fighting words"—words that can reasonably be considered an incitement or provocation toward physical conflict. Think about it: have you ever been embarrassed, upset, or saddened by words? The answer is likely yes. Words have power, and dealing with the negative emotions they generate—especially in a high-conflict divorce—is essential to maintaining your focus and composure.

Looking back, I realize I didn't seek help soon enough for what I was enduring. Over time, I came to understand that what I was doing to myself—internalizing the pain, guilt, and shame—was far worse than what had been done to me during the marriage. Even if you haven't experienced this level of abuse, it's likely that over the course of your marriage, you've developed certain habits, reactions, or mannerisms that won't serve you well in future relationships.

Since you're in a high-conflict divorce, it's important to acknowledge that some form of verbal, emotional, physical, or sexual abuse may have been present. Now, take a moment to think about that one thing your former spouse does—or did—that really irritates you.

1. How did you typically react?
2. How have you reacted during the divorce process?

3. How would you like to react?
4. Are any of those reactions emotionally healthy?

A healed person can acknowledge and convey their feelings without being overtaken by them. Part of your growth through this process will involve learning to regulate your emotions so they no longer control you. This is how you regain your strength and prepare yourself for healthier relationships in the future.

Individual counseling is essential when navigating divorce, especially in high-conflict situations. It provides a space to process the emotions and circumstances that led to your divorce, as well as those you're experiencing throughout the process. High-conflict divorces have a unique way of bringing out the worst in human nature, making it all the more critical to stay grounded. If you're overtaken by emotions, you risk missing opportunities to defend yourself and protect your children. Additionally, you'll need to break unhealthy habits before entering future relationships.

Ask yourself: "What habits or behaviors do I dislike about myself?" Seeking help for the pain and trauma you've endured is not a weakness; it's a sign of strength. It takes emotional maturity and responsibility to acknowledge, *I am damaged from my last relationship.* This is why you must take an introspective journey to heal yourself and, if you have children, to foster their healing as well. Your next relationship will benefit from the work you put into becoming a healthier version of yourself. I learned this the hard way—bringing bad habits from my first marriage into my next relationship.

Fortunately, my wife now appreciates the work I've done to improve.

To determine whether you need counseling, answer these questions honestly.

- If you can identify 10 issues, you need counseling.
- If you find 5, you need counseling.
- If you can pinpoint even 1, you still need counseling.
- And if you think you have none, you might be in denial.

In a 2022 *Psychology Today* article, Dr. Ann Buscho explained that while communication often fails in marriages, it remains essential in divorce—particularly in high-conflict cases, where effective communication becomes exponentially more important. To help manage communication, I recommend using a co-parenting app to document conversations, even if you don't have children. These apps remove ambiguity and provide a clear record of interactions, which can be critical in legal proceedings. A quick search in your phone's app store will provide several options.

Dr. Buscho also introduced an acronym for effective communication: **T.H.I.N.K.**

- **T**: Is it TRUE?
- **H**: Is it HELPFUL?
- **I**: Is it INSPIRING?
- **N**: Is it NECESSARY?
- **K**: Is it KIND?

You might find yourself thinking, *I can handle TRUE and NECESSARY, but HELPFUL, INSPIRING, and KIND? What's in it for me?* The answer is twofold.

1. You gain the ability to regulate your emotions, a skill that extends beyond your current situation to your relationships, career, and family.
2. If you have children, they get to see you handle conflict in a healthy, productive manner—a gift that benefits their development and future relationships.

Here's another HOT moment: You've probably heard the phrase, *Think twice.* I encourage you to take it literally. Read your messages twice before sending them. From experience, I can tell you this approach saved me from sending several messages that never should have reached my ex-wife's eyes. By the second read, my emotions were often more under control. Of course, it doesn't always work—high-conflict situations are inherently emotional, and I knew my ex-wife's triggers as well as she knew mine.

The final step in self-growth is accountability. Many people surround themselves with individuals who side with them, but what you truly need is someone willing to tell you the truth. High-conflict divorces are fueled by high emotions, and you need someone who can help you navigate those feelings rationally. I was fortunate to have people who played devil's advocate—my best friend, my future wife, and even some acquaintances. They would challenge me with questions like, "Why would she say or do that? What did you say to her? What role did you play?"

From Conflict to Clarity

They often offered suggestions like, "You shouldn't have said that; it's going to escalate the conversation. Maybe try this instead."

This level of accountability is invaluable, but it only works if you're willing to listen and apply the advice. As I mentioned earlier, in Texas, disrespectful behavior can land you in contempt of court. Thankfully, my ex-wife and I communicated mostly via text, which provided a written record of our exchanges. When I was dating my current wife, I would ask her to review my messages to ensure I wasn't coming across as overly emotional. Her feedback often helped me refine my tone and avoid unnecessary conflict. While some might consider this unnecessary, our premarital counselor, Paul Myers, called it a great idea— it removed impulsivity and fostered healthier communication.

Let me dispel a myth: non-emotional people are not free from emotions. Often, they are highly emotional individuals who suppress their feelings instead of expressing them. Emotional balance, however, involves hearing viewpoints you may disagree with and responding thoughtfully in stressful situations. Most high-conflict situations arise when one or more parties cannot act or react rationally. As much as it is within your sphere of control, you are responsible for managing your actions.

Take a moment to look at your current situation.

1) How did I contribute to the downfall of my marriage?

_____

_____

_____

_____

2). What negative habits do I need to change?

_____

_____

_____

_____

3). Why am I so bitter at my ex-spouse?

_____

_____

_____

_____

_____

4). Who will I hold myself accountable to that can tell me the truth on my growth?

_____

_____

_____

_____

Chapter 5
Help for Your Children

◈•••──────•••──────•••◈

hildren are often the overlooked victims in a divorce. Their entire world is being turned upside down, and while it's difficult for us as adults to manage our emotions, imagine how overwhelming it must be for them. If there is physical, verbal, or psychological abuse in the home, it's essential to leave and take the necessary steps to protect them. The damage caused by staying in such a situation is often worse than the initial separation. I know this firsthand. My children shared with me how difficult it was for them to reconcile the negative things they were told about me with the experiences they had when they were with me. Interestingly, it made them analyze the words and actions of both parents more critically.

Most children want their parents to stay together, even in dysfunctional households. For them, divorce feels like the death of their family. To you, it may feel like a zombie apocalypse—the relationship is over, but it's still "alive" in some toxic, flesh-eating form. If you're not careful, this analogy can become all too real for your children. Are you feasting on their emotions in pursuit of a vendetta? Children sense tension and frustration, just as we can sense the atmosphere in a room. Have you ever been around a couple and felt the underlying anger or bitterness even before knowing the cause? Children are just as perceptive, if not more so.

As valid as your feelings about your ex-spouse may be, it's critical to take a step back and consider what your children are experiencing. Their spiritual, mental, and physical well-being must take precedence over your personal grievances. If abuse is present, you have every right to approach the divorce protectively. But if it's a matter of disagreements and personal differences, I challenge you to look beyond your emotions and focus on how your actions are affecting the most vulnerable people involved—your children. They are losing their sense of normalcy, and even dysfunctional normalcy feels normal until someone teaches you otherwise. Counseling is vital to help your children grow beyond the dysfunction they're experiencing.

In a *Healthline* article, Ashley Marcin outlined 10 ways children are impacted by divorce, including anger, social withdrawal, academic struggles, separation anxiety, regression, depression, and even risky behaviors. I noticed many of these signs in my own children but didn't have the knowledge to address them at the time. I thought I was protecting them by avoiding conversations about the divorce, but I later realized that denying them a voice to process their emotions in an age-appropriate way was harmful.

Here are three questions every parent going through a divorce should ask:

1. What can I do to help my children process this divorce?
2. How will I get my children the support they need?
3. How will I communicate to my children about my ex-spouse?

If you haven't thought about these questions or developed a strategy to address them, now is the time to start. Divorce is traumatic for adults; for children, it's even more destabilizing. Listening to your children and allowing them to express their thoughts and feelings honestly—without exposing them to adult conflicts—can be one of the most effective ways to help them cope. As a child of divorce, I remember feeling like my dad was divorcing *me*. I thought I had done something wrong to make him leave. Years later, my own children told me they were being told I was leaving them, too. At first, I tried to comply with standing orders in Texas by saying as little as possible. I would tell them, "The truth will come out eventually," and assure them of my love. But my lack of communication allowed others to fill the silence, and my children were deeply affected during the first six months of the divorce. They began lashing out at me, and I realized I had to address what was happening honestly, but in a way that didn't disparage their mother.

When I started talking to them openly—age-appropriately—about what was happening, they began to form their own beliefs about the situation based on their experiences. This shift was transformative. Getting your children the support they need is just as important as being open with them. Counseling can help them process their feelings in a safe environment. While it may feel difficult to seek help due to pride or shame, doing so is one of the best decisions you can make for them. Counselors can also provide valuable legal support by documenting the children's feelings and experiences, which can be shared in court if it's in their best interest.

Finding the right counselor is crucial. Some counselors carry unconscious biases, which may influence how they engage with you, your ex-spouse, and your children. For example, I encountered counselors who were shocked to learn that I was the custodial parent, automatically assuming that the father wouldn't have primary custody. A great counselor, however, isn't there to pick sides but to help your family move forward. My parental facilitator, Dr. Threats, once said, "I am not here to pick sides but to help you figure out the right direction for YOUR family." Divorce doesn't end your family; it just redefines it.

The hardest task, by far, is deciding how you will communicate with your children about your ex-spouse. Most standing orders prohibit disparaging the other parent, and for good reason. Speaking negatively about your ex may feel cathartic in the moment, but it only hurts your children. My approach was simple: "Your mother loves you. I love you. We just can't love each other anymore."

Even when others spoke negatively about my ex-wife, I set boundaries. For instance, when my grandmother made an inappropriate comment about her, I told her in front of my children that such remarks weren't acceptable. I explained that if she couldn't respect this boundary, the children and I wouldn't visit anymore. This approach is difficult, but it's the right thing to do. When you file for divorce, the case is titled "In the interest of [your child's name]." It's not about you; it's about them. If you keep their best interests at heart, you will emerge from this process as a better parent and person.

Finally, ask yourself: "What do I want my children to say about me after the divorce is over?" Write down your answer and let it guide your actions.

This process will end, and you will have more life with them.

My dad/mom was

_____

_____

_____

_____

_____

_____

What negative behaviors have you seen your children exhibit?

_____

_____

_____

_____

_____

Research and list characteristics you would like to see in your child's counselor:

_____

_____

_____

_____

_____

What common phrase will you use when discussing sensitive issues about your ex-spouse? Having planned responses will help you when your emotions are high.

_____

_____

_____

_____

_____

Chapter 6
Help for Your Family

‹‹‹ ⊪──────•••──────⊪ ›››

D ivorce, particularly when children are involved, is a test of your resolve, your character, and your ability to manage complex emotions. One of the most important realizations you must come to is this: you and your former spouse are still family. That may be difficult to accept, but as Dr. Threats wisely said, "What is best for YOUR family?"

You might argue that you're not family anymore because of the divorce, but humor me for a moment. Your children are family to you, and they are also family to your ex-spouse. By proximity and connectivity, this makes you family in a redefined sense—what some might call "extended family." Like any extended family, there will be a need for engagement, communication, and a common goal: the well-being of your children.

You, your children, and your ex-spouse will benefit from family counseling. Counseling provides a safe space for your children to express their thoughts and feelings while helping all parties navigate the complexities of their new family structure. As a certified belief therapist and former teacher, I've seen firsthand the importance of addressing emotions and managing them effectively. If you've ever struggled with turning the other cheek, as I have, you know how challenging it can be to balance your emotions in high-conflict situations.

I'll share a personal example. My former brother-in-law invites me to his children's events when I have my kids and vice versa. For years, I avoided these gatherings because the atmosphere was toxic. I didn't want to ruin what should have been a joyous occasion for his family. When I explained that I would drop the kids off to avoid conflict, he told me, "You better stay. We are still family." That statement stuck with me. It reminded me that divorce doesn't erase family ties; it reshapes them.

You may believe that all your family will side with you and resent your ex-spouse, but this isn't always the case. Relationships often continue beyond the marriage, and pretending they don't exist can be harmful. Consider the long-term: graduations, weddings, the birth of grandchildren, and other life milestones. Will you see your ex-spouse as a zombie bent on destruction, or as a flawed human being like yourself, working to do what's best for the children? Your perception matters, and it profoundly impacts your children.

Divorce isn't just the end of a marriage; it's the death of many aspects of your life. You're losing a shared future, extended family connections, and even friendships formed during your marriage. This is especially true in contentious divorces, where bitterness often creates a "loyalty test" for family and friends. It's a grieving process, not just for you but for everyone involved. When children are part of the equation, the stakes are even higher. Divorce becomes a disaster zone, leaving casualties in its wake if handled poorly. As you navigate this process, ask yourself: "What am I fighting over? How much value does this really have?" While assets are governed by the state, children are a different matter entirely. Children are not assets to be divided; they are individuals who are deeply affected by the actions of both parents.

Unlike dividing assets, separating children from the dynamics of divorce is impossible. Children are the glue that binds you to your ex-spouse forever, or at least until one of you is no longer alive. This connection can be messy and painful, but it is also unbreakable. Younger children are like wet glue—easier to separate with minimal damage but still messy. Older children, however, are like dried glue: separating them from the dynamics of divorce often causes permanent damage to both the glue and the paper it binds.

Children absorb the traits and emotions of their parents, making it even more critical for you to model healthy behavior. If you focus on vengeance or material gains, your children will internalize that conflict, and it will shape their future relationships. Instead, prioritize their emotional well-being and stability.

When my divorce began, my children were 12, almost 10, 2, and 1. The youngest two barely noticed the changes, but the older two were profoundly affected. My younger children simply asked, "Why aren't you home, Daddy?" It broke my heart, but I assured them their mother and I loved them, even if we couldn't live together anymore.

For my older children, the separation was far more damaging. They were caught in the emotional crossfire, hearing conflicting narratives from both parents. I made it a point to avoid disparaging their mother and instead focused on showing them love and support. I encouraged them to express their feelings and ensured they had access to counseling. This helped them process the divorce and develop their own understanding of what was happening.

For older children, the relationship between parents becomes less like glue and more like sand and water. Imagine two bottles of sand, one representing you and the other your ex-spouse, poured into a larger bottle. The sand blends together, representing shared experiences, emotions, and relationships. Now add water, symbolizing the children, which binds the sand even more tightly. Separating sand and water is impossible without causing significant damage to both.

Older children are more aware of family dynamics and can form their own opinions about what has occurred. Their schedules are busier, and they often have to navigate conflicting loyalties between parents. This is why effective communication and cooperation are crucial. Unfortunately, in my case, communication with my ex-wife often broke down, leading to missed opportunities for my children. Despite my efforts to prioritize their activities, conflicts sometimes made it impossible for them to participate.

If you're in a high-conflict divorce, you must make a conscious decision to lead with love, foresight, and character. Your children are your legacy—not your assets, career, or accolades. The damage you inflict on them during this process will shape their future relationships and emotional health. You have the power to influence this outcome by focusing on healing and growth.

Divorce with children is a natural disaster. It is messy, painful, and often feels insurmountable. But if you approach it with intentionality and compassion, you can minimize the damage and create a better future for your family. In the following chapters, we will explore strategies to help you heal, both for yourself and your children. For now, take a moment for self-reflection. Ask yourself: "What can I do to lead my family through this storm with integrity and love?"

Name the items that CAN be separated:

_____

_____

_____

_____

41

Name the items that CAN NOT be separated:

_____

_____

_____

_____

_____

How can you shift your attitude to make the environment better?

_____

_____

_____

_____

Chapter 7
Custody and New Family

C ustody is one of the most sensitive and complex aspects of a divorce, and it's determined by the judge in your case. Unfortunately, many people don't give it the thought it deserves until they're already in the thick of it. If you're reading this, chances are you're navigating a high-conflict divorce, so I want to share some insights I've gained from my experience to help you think ahead and avoid common pitfalls. Custody isn't just about who gets the kids when; it's about creating a framework that serves the best interests of your children while protecting your peace and sanity.

Here are a few key considerations when establishing custody:

1. Is the drop-off and pickup location consistent?
2. How long do you wait before leaving the agreed drop-off location?
3. How do you handle teenagers who don't want to visit?

4. How will you handle celebrations?
5. When and how will you introduce children to new partners?
6. What role will bonus (step) parents play in the children's lives?

These might seem like minor logistical details, but trust me, they can become major pain points in a high-conflict situation. Let's break this down further.

What happens if drop-offs and pickups occur at each other's homes? On the surface, this seems convenient, but if conflict arises, your home—your place of peace and safety—is suddenly exposed to unnecessary tension. I recommend choosing a neutral, high-traffic, centralized location for exchanges. This keeps the drama away from your home and creates a safer environment for everyone involved.

Habitually late or canceled visitation can be a nightmare for the custodial parent. My ex-wife often let me know just one day before her visitation that she wasn't going to take the kids, even though she had informed the children weeks earlier. This threw my plans into chaos and disrupted the children's expectations. To prevent this, ask the judge to specify how much advance notice is required to cancel visitation. In many cases, the parent with visitation is also responsible for arranging childcare if they can't be present. Additionally, keep a detailed record of all missed or canceled visits. This documentation will be invaluable if custody modifications arise later.

This is one of the most challenging issues to address. Legally, you're obligated to make your child available for the other parent, even if they refuse to go. My 17-year-old daughter, who has dealt with trauma involving her mother, refuses visitation. Forcing her to go puts me in a precarious situation: if she resists physically and gets bruised or scratched, I could be accused of abuse. In these cases, I consulted both my lawyer and CPS to clarify my obligations. If there are genuine safety concerns, you can request a restraining order, but substantial evidence is required. Counseling can also help the child and the other parent work through these issues together.

Celebrations are tough. In Texas, the non-custodial parent is entitled to two hours of visitation on the child's birthday if it doesn't fall on their custodial day. For children, this can feel like a fragmented celebration, as they often wish both parents could be present. If possible, work with your ex to create a shared plan for birthdays and milestones. This isn't easy, especially if emotions are running high, but it's one of those moments where you have to set aside your differences and focus on what's best for the kids. If this feels impossible, talk to a counselor or someone you trust to help you process your feelings and identify ways to move forward.

Introducing children to a new partner requires careful consideration. It's not just about you and your excitement over a new relationship; it's about how your children feel and whether they're ready. I recommend waiting at least six months before introducing your kids to someone you're dating. This gives you time to evaluate the relationship and ensures your children have had space to heal from the divorce. When I started dating my now-wife, I waited about 5-6 months before introducing her to my children. By then, I was confident that she was someone I wanted in my life long-term. Fortunately, my kids welcomed her, and her children were receptive to me as well. Rushing this step can create resentment and damage both your new relationship and your children's trust.

The dynamic between step-parents and children can be tricky. In our blended family counseling, our counselor advised that the biological parent should handle most discipline while the step-parent focuses on building bonds with the children. This requires clear and frequent communication between you and your spouse to establish boundaries and expectations. For instance, if your spouse has issues with something your children are doing, it's your job to address it with your kids. However, step-parents can and should correct behaviors that directly affect them, such as disrespect. It takes intentional effort, but this approach helps build stronger relationships while reducing conflict.

This strategy also protects you legally. During my custody modification, opposing counsel questioned whether my wife disciplined my children. If the answer had been yes, it could have been used against me in court. Remember, anyone who interacts with your children because of your relationship can either help or hinder your case. It's crucial to think ahead and be intentional about how you navigate these dynamics.

Custody arrangements are about more than just schedules; they're about creating stability and minimizing conflict for your children. The decisions you make now will have long-lasting impacts on their well-being and your relationship with them. Take the time to think through these details, communicate effectively, and put your children's best interests at the forefront of every decision. You won't regret it.

Chapter 8
Reimbursements

Reimbursement is typically itemized in your decree as any out-of-pocket expenses incurred for your children's medical and dental care. It's essential to keep all receipts and share them with your ex-spouse within the designated timeframe outlined in your decree to ensure you receive the reimbursement. Missing this window could result in losing your claim to those expenses. Many people overlook this detail, but meticulous documentation can save you significant time, money, and stress.

Here's where most people miss the mark: while medical and dental expenses are commonly covered, you can also request that the judge include educational expenses and extracurricular activities in the decree. In some states, these costs are automatically included, but in Texas, it's up to the judge's discretion. If you don't address these during the divorce or modification process, you may find yourself solely responsible for these costs down the line.

For example, in my case, my ex-wife initially agreed to support all extracurricular activities, but for seven years, she provided no financial support for them. During our modification hearing, she asked that whichever parent signed the children up for an activity should bear the cost unless both parties agreed beforehand. The judge sided with her, ruling that the non-signing parent would not be responsible for any activity the other parent initiated without mutual consent. This outcome placed the full burden of funding activities like golf, culinary classes, baseball, and gymnastics squarely on me. Child support alone isn't sufficient to cover these additional expenses, so it's crucial to plan ahead.

When preparing for your divorce or modification, here are some key steps to consider:

1. **Be Proactive in Negotiations**: Make sure to bring up extracurricular and educational expenses during negotiations or mediation. Provide examples of your children's current or anticipated activities and highlight their importance to the children's growth and well-being. Judges are more likely to approve these expenses when presented with a clear and reasonable explanation.

2. **Request Specificity in Your Decree**: Don't settle for vague language. If possible, have your lawyer include explicit details about how these expenses will be divided. For instance, "Extracurricular

activities agreed upon by both parents will be split 50/50, and each parent must provide written consent before enrollment." This ensures clarity and accountability.

3. **Track Everything**: Keep meticulous records of all expenses. Use a spreadsheet to log the date, purpose, and amount of each expense. Attach receipts, invoices, and any related documentation. Make sure to keep copies of communications where these expenses were discussed. This not only protects you legally but also provides transparency if disputes arise.

4. **Submit Requests Promptly**: Many decrees require reimbursement requests to be submitted within a specific timeframe, often 30 days. Missing this window can mean forfeiting your right to reimbursement. Set reminders or use apps to track deadlines.

5. **Be Prepared to Negotiate**: If your ex-spouse disputes an expense, be ready to provide context and documentation. Stay calm and focused on the children's needs during these discussions, as emotional reactions can hinder resolution.

As your friend in this process, let me tell you: advocating for your children's needs while navigating a contentious divorce can be exhausting, but it's worth it. These activities—whether they're sports, music lessons, or academic enrichment programs—provide structure and normalcy for your children during an otherwise chaotic time. They also show your kids that their passions and interests are valued, which is critical to their emotional well-being.

If you find yourself in a situation where your ex-spouse refuses to contribute, don't hesitate to revisit the issue in a modification. Circumstances can change, and judges will often reconsider terms if there's a clear benefit to the children.

Finally, remember that documentation isn't just about protecting yourself; it's about fairness. By keeping detailed records and submitting them on time, you're showing the court that you're organized, cooperative, and focused on your children's best interests. That kind of credibility can go a long way in future legal proceedings.

If this seems overwhelming, know that you're not alone. Every step you take toward organization and advocacy is a step closer to ensuring your children have the resources and opportunities they deserve.

Chapter 9
Communication

━━━━━━━━━━━━

If you're reading this book, it likely means you've experienced—or are currently experiencing—the hostile nature of dealing with a former spouse during or after a high-conflict divorce. As I mentioned earlier, unless something drastic happens, you'll have to navigate communication with this person until one of you is no longer here. While communication often decreases significantly when your child turns 18, until then, it remains an ongoing and necessary part of co-parenting.

If you're relying on verbal communication with your former spouse, you're setting yourself up for potential discord and unnecessary confusion. Words spoken in frustration or misunderstanding can easily be twisted or forgotten, and that ambiguity creates fertile ground for conflict. To reduce the chance of miscommunication and protect yourself, I strongly recommend using communication software. There are several excellent options available, each designed to simplify the logistical and emotional complexities of co-parenting. These tools provide benefits like scheduling notifications for events, submitting receipts, and requesting or tracking payments. More importantly, they create a clear and comprehensive record of every interaction—records that are admissible in court should any disputes arise.

Perhaps one of the greatest advantages of these apps is that they allow you to maintain necessary communication without engaging in verbal arguments or emotionally charged conversations with someone you disagree with. This buffer can save you countless headaches while ensuring that you remain focused on what truly matters: your children and their well-being.

Let me share how this has helped me personally. During my modification hearing, my ex-wife's lawyer tried to claim that I had cursed at her and called her names. They even presented a snippet of a message from the parenting app to support their claim. However, they conveniently omitted the full context of our exchange. In the message, I had written, "My grandmother died last week, and my mother is in the hospital sick. I don't have time for your drama. Leave me the ___ alone." When her lawyer asked me about the timing of this message, my lawyer quickly pulled up the entire conversation from the app, showing not only the full context but also the pattern of misrepresentation.

This scenario played out multiple times during my testimony. Without the app, I wouldn't have had the documentation to back up the truth. That's why I can't emphasize enough: do not make agreements or communicate anything of substance over the phone. When you communicate verbally, your words are fleeting, and their interpretation can be easily manipulated. Written communication allows you to pause, reflect, and ensure you're articulating your thoughts accurately. It also gives you a chance to remove emotional language and replace it with what's right and necessary.

Here's another key point: when words come out of your mouth, you can't take them back. But when something is in writing, you can edit it before hitting send. Writing helps you process your feelings and ensures you're presenting yourself in the best possible light. Parenting apps provide that critical layer of protection and clarity, and they've been essential in my personal experience.

As we wrap up this section, I want to leave you with the most valuable lessons I've learned from the tragedy of my divorce. These lessons have become my guiding principles, and I hope they'll help you as well:

1. **Be honest.** Honesty builds credibility and keeps you grounded.
2. **Find the right lawyer.** The right legal representation can change everything.
3. **Get help—for yourself, your children, and your family.** Healing is a process that requires professional support.
4. **Track your assets.** Documentation is your best defense in court.

5. **Use a communication app.** It's not just practical; it's a lifesaver in high-conflict situations.

Every divorce is unique, but the principles for navigating them successfully remain the same. Use this space to jot down any strategies you want to implement or questions you still need to address. I hope the insights in this book provide clarity, strength, and guidance as you move forward. You've got this, and I wish you the best of luck on your journey.

Sincerely,

Edwin Gray

Read the Divorce Paperwork Thoroughly

_____

_____

_____

_____

The Right Lawyer and Your Responses

_____

_____

_____

_____

Division of Assets

_____

_____

_____

_____

Help for Myself

_____

_____

_____

_____

Help for Your Children

_____

_____

_____

_____

Division of Children

_____

_____

_____

_____

Custody and New Family

_____

_____

_____

_____

Reimbursements

_____

_____

_____

_____

Index

❧ ⊪———— •••————⊪ ❦

General Resources

1. Legal Services Corporation (LSC)

- Website: www.lsc.gov
- LSC funds local legal aid organizations that provide free legal help for low-income families. Use their search tool to find legal aid offices in your state or region.

2. American Bar Association (ABA)

- Website: www.americanbar.org
- The ABA offers resources and a lawyer referral service. Their Find Legal Help tool provides links to local and state legal aid offices.

3. LawHelp.org

- Website: www.lawhelp.org
- LawHelp connects individuals to free legal aid programs in their area. It also includes information on family law issues like custody, divorce, and child support.

4. State or County Bar Association

- Many state and local bar associations have lawyer referral services and legal aid resources. Check your state or county bar association's website for family law-specific help.

5. Local Legal Aid Offices

- Search for legal aid offices in your county or city. These organizations often focus on family law, including custody, divorce, and child support cases.

6. Pro Bono Programs

- Many law firms and legal organizations offer pro bono (free) services for individuals with low income. Contact local law schools, bar associations, or legal aid offices for information on pro bono programs in your area.

7. Online Legal Platforms

- Websites like Avvo (www.avvo.com) and Justia (www.justia.com) allow you to search for family law attorneys in your area and often provide options for free consultations.

8. 211 Helpline

- Dial 211 or visit www.211.org to connect with local services, including legal aid for family law issues.

9. Court Self-Help Centers

- Many family courts have self-help centers or clinics that provide free legal information, forms, and guidance for family law matters. Contact your local family court for details.

American Bar Association Directory:

https://www.americanbar.org/groups/legal_services/flh-home/flh-free-legal-help/.

Resources by State

Alabama

- Legal Services Alabama
  - Phone: (866) 456-4995
  - Website: https://www.legalservicesalabama.org/

Alaska

- Alaska Legal Services Corporation
  - Phone: (888) 478-2572
  - Website: https://www.alsc-law.org/

Arizona

- Community Legal Services
  - Phone: (800) 852-9075
  - Website: https://clsaz.org/

Arkansas

- Center for Arkansas Legal Services
  - Phone: (800) 950-5817
  - Website: https://www.arlegalservices.org/

California

- Legal Aid Foundation of Los Angeles
  - Phone: (800) 399-4529
  - Website: https://lafla.org/

Colorado

- Colorado Legal Services
  - Phone: (303) 837-1321

- o Website: https://www.coloradolegalservices.org/

Connecticut

- Statewide Legal Services of Connecticut
  - o Phone: (800) 453-3320
  - o Website: https://slsct.org/

Delaware

- Legal Services Corporation of Delaware
  - o Phone: (302) 575-0408
  - o Website: https://lscd.com/

Florida

- Legal Services of Greater Miami
  - o Phone: (305) 576-0080
  - o Website: https://legalservicesmiami.org/

Georgia

- Georgia Legal Services Program
  - o Phone: (833) 457-7529
  - o Website: https://www.glsp.org/

Hawaii

- Legal Aid Society of Hawaii
  - o Phone: (800) 499-4302
  - o Website: https://www.legalaidhawaii.org/

Idaho

- Idaho Legal Aid Services
  - o Phone: (208) 746-7541
  - o Website: https://www.idaholegalaid.org/

Illinois

- Land of Lincoln Legal Aid
  - Phone: (877) 342-7891
  - Website: https://lincolnlegal.org/

Indiana

- Indiana Legal Services
  - Phone: (844) 243-8570
  - Website: https://www.indianalegalservices.org/

Iowa

- Iowa Legal Aid
  - Phone: (800) 532-1275
  - Website: https://www.iowalegalaid.org/

Kansas

- Kansas Legal Services
  - Phone: (800) 723-6953
  - Website: https://www.kansaslegalservices.org/

Kentucky

- Legal Aid of the Bluegrass
  - Phone: (859) 431-8200
  - Website: https://lablaw.org/

Louisiana

- Southeast Louisiana Legal Services
  - Phone: (877) 521-6242
  - Website: https://slls.org/

Maine

- Pine Tree Legal Assistance
  - Phone: (207) 774-8211
  - Website: https://ptla.org/

Maryland

- Maryland Legal Aid
  - Phone: (410) 951-7777
  - Website: https://www.mdlab.org/

Massachusetts

- Greater Boston Legal Services
  - Phone: (617) 371-1234
  - Website: https://www.gbls.org/

Michigan

- Legal Aid of Western Michigan
  - Phone: (616) 774-0672
  - Website: https://lawestmi.org/

Minnesota

- Legal Aid Service of Northeastern Minnesota
  - Phone: (800) 933-1112
  - Website: https://lasnem.org/

Mississippi

- Mississippi Center for Legal Services
  - Phone: (800) 498-1804
  - Website: https://mscenterforlegalservices.org/

Missouri

- Legal Services of Eastern Missouri

- o Phone: (314) 534-4200
- o Website: https://lsem.org/

Montana

- Montana Legal Services Association
  - o Phone: (800) 666-6899
  - o Website: https://www.mtlsa.org/

Nebraska

- Legal Aid of Nebraska
  - o Phone: (877) 250-2016
  - o Website: https://www.legalaidofnebraska.org/

Nevada

- Nevada Legal Services
  - o Phone: (702) 386-0404
  - o Website: https://nlslaw.net/

New Hampshire

- New Hampshire Legal Assistance
  - o Phone: (800) 639-5290
  - o Website: https://www.nhla.org/

New Jersey

- Legal Services of New Jersey
  - o Phone: (888) 576-5529
  - o Website: https://www.lsnj.org/

New Mexico

- New Mexico Legal Aid
  - o Phone: (833) 545-4357
  - o Website: https://www.newmexicolegalaid.org/

New York

- Legal Aid Society
  - Phone: (212) 577-3300
  - Website: https://legalaidnyc.org/

References

Revealing Divorce Statistics In 2023. Aug 2023;
https://www.forbes.com/advisor/legal/divorce/divorce-
statistics/

Marcin, Ashley, 10 Effects of Divorce on Children — and
Helping Them Cope, May 2020,
https://www.healthline.com/health/parenting/effects-of-
divorce-on-children

Clin Child Fam Psychol Rev. 2002 Sep; 5(3): 173–195,
https://www.ncbi.nlm.nih.gov/pmc/articles/PMC3161510/

Edwin B. Gray

"Divorce is hard. Navigating it doesn't have to be."

Packed with honest advice and practical strategies, this concise guide helps you tackle the emotional, legal, and logistical challenges of divorce. From understanding custody to managing finances and communication, discover tools to protect your sanity, prioritize your children, and rebuild your life. Your future starts here.

www.ingramcontent.com/pod-product-compliance
Lightning Source LLC
Chambersburg PA
CBHW060351050426
42449CB00011B/2932